Angela D. Oliphant

EMERGING INTO YOUR WHOLE & BEAUTIFUL LIFE!

21 Days of Devotion and Journaling

Studio Griffin
A Publishing Company
www.studiogriffin.net

Emerging Into Your Whole & Beautiful Life!
21 Days of Devotion and Journaling
Copyright © 2020 Angela D. Oliphant

All Rights Reserved. No part of this book may be used or reproduced in any manner whatsoever without written permission except in the case of brief quotations embodied in critical articles and reviews.

For information, contact:

Studio Griffin
A Publishing Company
Garner, North Carolina
studiogriffin@outlook.com
www.studiogriffin.net

Cover Design by Ruth E. Griffin
Image by © nirutft

Unless otherwise indicated, all Scripture taken from taken from The Holy Bible, King James Version. New York: American Bible Society: 1999.

First Edition

ISBN-13: 978-1-7351353-3-5

Library of Congress Control Number: 2020913287

1 2 3 4 5 6 7 8 9 10

I would like to dedicate this book to my family by blood and by connection who always knew I had the gift of speaking and writing long before I knew it and recognized it for myself.

TABLE OF CONTENTS

Introduction	1
Your Whole and Beautiful Life	5
Day One: Ruth	7
Day Two: The Samaritan Woman	11
Day Three: Abigail	15
Day Four: The Woman With The Issue	19
Day Five: Rahab	24
Day Six: The Servant Girl	29
Day Seven: The Woman With An Infirmity	32
Day Eight: Esther	35
Day Nine: Hannah	38
Day Ten: Daughters of Zelophehad	41
Day Eleven: Mary, The Mother of Jesus	44
Day Twelve: Deborah	47
Day Thirteen: Rizpah	50
Day Fourteen: Gomer	53
Day Fifteen: Leah	57
Day Sixteen: Hagar	60
Day Seventeen: Lydia	64
Day Eighteen: Angela Denise	67
Day Nineteen: Confidence	71
Day Twenty: Write Your Story	74
Day Twenty-One: Connection	77
Decisions	80
Poem	83
Acknowledgement	87
About the Author	89

EMERGING INTO YOUR WHOLE & BEAUTIFUL LIFE!

21 Days of Devotion and Journaling

ೞ INTRODUCTION ೦ಌ

EMErging is something we all do at some point in our lives if we desire to move forward. Life is a journey, and in that journey comes many transitions which cause us to eMErge. For some, it happens easily. For others, it happens later. It doesn't matter the age you are when it occurs. What matters is that you embrace the eMErging and allow yourself to come forth, transition, and be transformed. The process in most cases will not be easy. It may be a struggle and will take some strength—mentally, spiritually, and physically. But at the end of it all (which truly is your beginning), it will be well worth the struggle and will supersede the fight inside that shell to break through to finally come out of the shadows, obscurity, and darkness; and shine forth with the light that was inside of you all along.

This light will shine brighter than any other moment you have experienced because in this light the authentic YOU will finally be released, and you will have eMErged! We all have gifts that we embody, things we do well and love to do, even things we may not even know that are a part of us because it has never been tapped into. Maybe we have lived our lives trying to shine from someone else's light; a light they said was out but, as we grew and matured, we found out it was their light all along. Just think about trying to fulfill someone else's dream, believing that it was your dream too. Then realizing this is not me, this is not my heart's desire, this has never been MY dream. At that point your threshing floor experience, your eMErging has just begun.

As I said earlier, eMErging is a process. Webster's dictionary defines it as gradual changes that lead toward a particular result. It may take days, months, and even years. The good thing about it is we get to decide! If we fight against the process, it will take a lifetime and at the end you still would not have eMErged. Once we embrace it, accept it, and yield to the process though, things can happen very quickly. During the process it is rarely recognized or even realized that we are going through changes. You see it as life happening to you and begin to ask why, how? No thought or consideration arises in us to say, "Hey, I'm walking through this process that's going to lead me to a particular result." This eMErging will be a struggle and it will seem as though you're in a dark place but that is the place where you are being developed. There are things that you need to address and handle in your life that only you can do. This place may feel like a lonely place with no one to assist or help, but know this: you are never really alone.

The eMErging process can be compared to a baby chick breaking forth from the egg or a caterpillar going through its' struggle in the cocoon to become a beautiful butterfly. The transition to become is a real event and you have to be watchful, careful and meticulous during the time of your transition. When you are in transition, you are at your most vulnerable state. That's why the baby chick has the egg shell and the caterpillar has the cocoon. You must look out for yourself and be self-aware as you are becoming what and who you know you should be. It's a time of evaluation and planning. It takes twenty-one days for a baby chick to transform, hatch and break out of its shell. It takes a caterpillar twenty-eight to thirty-eight days for it to convert itself into a butterfly. In my research, I discovered that by expert's opinion, it takes twenty-one days to change a habit or behavior and it takes at least thirteen positive things being said to cancel only one negative thing. That discovery has led me to believe this: I have to always speak positively to myself and to guard and protect myself from the negative. I must encourage myself, be kind to myself, and love myself. I have to be my own cheerleader! If no one else will fight for me or push me forward, I must do it for myself. My eMErgence depends on ME! Yes, it is a process, but I am well worth the journey, the blood, sweat, tears and the time! The only thing that is holding you back is YOU! Release yourself, live on purpose and EMERGE!

In the upcoming chapters of this book, we will embark upon a journey into some women's lives that will literally change your life forever. Some of them are

Biblical women, but I want you to see them just as any other woman with struggles and decisions to make. Their stories are what I want you to see. These are real women with real issues, and each had to make the decision to eMErge to become what they knew in their heart they could be. So get ready to be challenged and to be changed because within these pages you will not only glean from the women who have gone before you, but my prayer and heart's desire is that you find yourself on the pages and you too will come to the realization that it is time for you to EMERGE!

ꙮ YOUR WHOLE AND ꙮ BEAUTIFUL LIFE

Being whole and beautiful is not about having the perfect life—it is a state of mind. It's about information, revelation, and change. It is about you as an individual seeking out what you need to eMErge into the vision you already have in your heart. It's about making the connections and seeing your dreams come true; holding on to what you believe for yourself and not letting anyone or anything deter you from what you believe is your purpose and what you know is your passion! To be whole means being healed—not so much that you are already healed but you are in the process of being healed, of having all your proper parts and components. To be beautiful means excellent, very good of its kind, having the qualities of beauty, grace, attractive, and pleasing. The list goes on and on. But your 'beautiful' may not be my 'beautiful' and that is fine because our lives are not meant to touch everybody; they will touch somebody and the first somebody should be us.

The pictures that are posted online usually don't show forth the true aspect of people's lives. These pictures could be altered, filtered, or edited, giving a "sense" of reality. Being authentic is rare and that's the beauty of it. When we are real and honest with ourselves and others, our whole and beautiful life will shine through. Truth causes us to be whole and brings forth our inner most beauty.

There is a beauty that lies within our situations and circumstances. I would even say it lies within our hard places. For the majority of us, we can't see that beauty because we focus on the issue. But if we could just step back and look at everything objectively, we would realize that no matter how hard or difficult things may be, something beautiful and something meaningful will come out of this! That this mistake can be my miracle, this hardship can be helpful, and this tragedy can indeed be my triumph! Often time's things are not seen in this manner, it is so much easier to be negative, but we must begin to change our mindsets and start seeing victory even in the midst of defeat.

What is holding you up from eMErging into your whole and beautiful life? Who or what put you in a box and caused you to fear, so you allow the box to confine you? Today is the day you need to destroy that box and break free. You may be wounded but wounds can heal. You may be broken but you can be mended. The question is, how bad do you want it? And whatever 'it' is for you, what are you willing to do to get it? You've been given this awesome opportunity called life, so embrace it, eMErge and do your best to make it whole and beautiful!

ಜಿ Day 1 ೡ
RUTH

And Ruth said, Intreat me not to leave thee,
or to return from following after thee: for whither
thou goest, I will go; and where thou lodgest,
I will lodge: thy people shall be my people,
and thy God my God.
Ruth 1:16

Ruth was a widow. Her husband had passed away, along with his brother and father. At that point, Ruth could have gone back to her homeland and started her life over amongst her relatives, but she didn't. She seized the moment to stay with her mother in-law, Naomi. and take care of her. She saw this moment as an opportunity to become, to change, to do something different and not return to the familiar. Where others would have perceived this as a death sentence, she saw an awesome opportunity.

Ruth was from Moab, a kingdom of ancient Palestine. Her people came from among the Israelites and began living their lives outside of where God desired that they be. Where they once stood with Israel, now they were opposed to it. She knew what it was like to be a follower of the Most High God and she knew what it was like to walk away and oppose Him too.

At the time of Ruth's husband's death, widows were treated as less than, as if they were worthless to society. It was the responsibility of the husband's brother or other male members of his family to take care of the widow, but there was no male left to take care of her due to her husband, her brother in-law, and her father in-law passing away at the same time. Ruth was placed in a situation where she had to decide what to do with her life and it wasn't an easy decision to make. She could go back to where she came from which would be a familiar lifestyle for her; or she could stay with her mother-in-law and move forward to the unknown.

In the end, Ruth made the decision to go with Naomi. She knew well where she came from, but for her going back wasn't an option. She couldn't change the fact that her husband had passed away, but she could change the direction of her own life.

However, Naomi did not offer her an opportunity or a chance to go with her. Naomi told Ruth and her other daughter-in-law, Orpah, that they should go back to their homes, marry again, have children, and make a life in Moab. But Ruth said, "No, I'm going to stay with you." She had bonded with Naomi and didn't want to leave her side. She stayed with her to take care of her and serve and worship her God. Nothing or no one could deter her—her mind was made up, so she said goodbye to Orpah, and she left with Naomi.

This was the beginning of her eMErging! This was not an instantaneous decision—it took time for her to make the decision she felt was right for her. Ruth had to do things she hadn't done before: she had to think differently and move differently. She also had to embrace the process, the awkwardness, and the transition into her new life, disregarding how it all felt. Feelings had nothing to do with this—she was reaching for her destiny even though she had no idea what that destiny would be. She didn't have the details, she just had the heart to see it through to the end.

Through her eMErging, she became the wife of a man who loved and cared for her and Naomi. Life wasn't easy for her, but she pushed through the hard times and allowed every trial and every hurt to build her up and assist her into her eMErging.

Sometimes we can't see the end of a thing; we just have to trust the process!

In your life now, what thing do you have to trust the process in? What are you doing to help you trust the process?

ᛞ Day 2 ᛤ
THE SAMARITAN WOMAN

*Then saith the woman of Samaria unto him,
How is it that thou, being a Jew, askest drink of me,
which am a woman of Samaria? For the Jews have no
dealings with the Samaritans.
John 4:9*

The Samaritan woman was knowledgeable of the law of God. She was intelligent and articulate, yet she had an emptiness in her that went unfulfilled. Jesus said she had five husbands and the one she was with at that time wasn't her husband. The Bible doesn't mention what happened to her husbands: did they pass away from some kind of illness? Were they killed in a war? Did they just up and leave her one day? Or did she leave them in hopes of finding someone better?

Her mention in John 4 gives us some insight into her life. Through her responses and statements, we see that she was a woman who studied and learned the law. She was a woman of great strength and yet at the same time, she was weak: she didn't like being alone. She had street smarts and good ole' fashioned common sense, but emotionally she was a wreck. It seems as though she thought that she couldn't make it or be who she wanted to be unless she had a man in her life. This is somewhat understandable due to the culture she lived in and because she was a part of what was considered to be a mixed generation, who were looked down upon. The Samaritan woman had learned to be quick with her words and her responses. I believe she did this because she had to, not because it was a part of who she was growing up. She had to eMErge to protect herself but when Jesus came along she had a rebirth, a time to eMErge again. This time when she eMErged, it was with the right perspective, the right attitude, and the right heart. The love that Jesus gave her that day at the well caused her to see herself for the first time. It destroyed the things that had her bound, and she now was able to be truly free! So free that she went running through the streets telling people to come see a MAN who literally changed her life forever!

eMErging for her seemed to be a quick shift. One, because she had done it before to some degree; and two, she was ready and embraced the change. She never denied her past, or her present, nor did she try to cover it up. She was open and transparent with Jesus. She was at the end of her transition and ready to walk through the process, it was time for her to eMErge. We don't know what she went on to do in her life, but we do know that she was free, and that freedom caused her to share with others so they also could be free.

Emerging Into Your Whole & Beautiful Life

An encounter with TRUTH can change your life forever and for the better!

What is your truth? How can you embrace it and allow it to have a positive impact on your life?

_____
_____
_____
_____
_____
_____
_____
_____
_____
_____
_____
_____
_____
_____
_____
_____
_____
_____

๛ Day 3 ๖
ABIGAIL

Now the name of the man was Nabal; and the name of his wife Abigail: and she was a woman of good understanding, and of a beautiful countenance: but the man was churlish and evil in his doings; and he was of the house of Caleb.
1 Samuel 25:3

Abigail's name means, the Father's Joy! What a powerful definition. It doesn't just mean joy but the Father's Joy which makes it a noun and tangible. It's not just a description of her, it is her! This is why I personally believe we all should be careful when naming our children: it's not just a name, you are prophesying their future. Every time you call their name you are decreeing and declaring into the atmosphere who they are and who they will become. Names are powerful whether good or bad. We have what we say, what we speak so make sure you speak life over your seed!

So here is Abigail, the Father's Joy, married to Nabal, who, according to scripture, is a mean man. His name denotes foolishness, surliness, and wickedness. Nabal was a drunk who didn't treat his wife well, but he was wealthy. Abigail may not have wanted for any material thing in life, she may have had all she could ever ask for in the natural sense but Nabal didn't care for her spiritually and emotionally. He didn't love her like a husband should love his wife. The Bible commands husbands to love their wives even as Christ loved the church and gave Himself (Ephesians 5:25), but this was not the case with Nabal and Abigail.

Being the wicked man that he is, Nabal ends up in a situation where he dishonors a man of God by the name of David. Because of this disgrace, David makes it known that Nabal and his family will pay. Abigail receives word that her family is in danger of losing their lives due to Nabal's actions, so she acts to stop the course of evil that is headed her way. Due to her quick thinking and quick moving, she is able to save herself and her entire household, including Nabal.

Through this situation, Abigail eMErged. She didn't operate out of bitterness, anger or even rage. She looked at the situation as an opportunity. When we read her story, we see that she was respected by her servants because they didn't hesitate to act when she spoke to them. They didn't fight against her. She was a woman who was honored by those who were her servants. To me, this says she carried herself with dignity and respect.

Although Abigail physically was still married to Nabal, her mind was already out of the marriage. Her perspective was outside of the limits and boundaries that were set up around her. When this situation occurred, she didn't hesitate. She didn't have time to try to figure things out. After saving herself and her household, she had to go back home to Nabal and his wickedness, surliness, and alcoholism. Her eMErging didn't immediately change her circumstances. When she arrived home, she still had a husband who was partying, drinking and had no knowledge of her leaving or returning.

In spite of all that, God honored Abigail. After she eMErged and took this huge step, she was set up for her future. Later in life, her husband, Nabal, passed away and Abigail then became the wife of David, the King. She wasn't looking to be his wife, she was just doing what needed to be done only to end up living as the King's wife.

Your unfavorable situation or circumstance should never determine your future, be the change you need!

How can you be the change that you need? What steps could you take to become the answer to your problem?

___
___
___
___
___
___
___
___
___
___
___
___
___
___
___
___
___
___
___
___

೮ Day 4 ೞ
THE WOMAN WITH THE ISSUE

And, behold, a woman, which was diseased with an issue of blood twelve years, came behind him, and touched the hem of his garment.
Matthew 9:20

This verse tells us just what we need to know about this woman. The first thing we learn about her is that she had an issue. But she didn't just have an issue, she was diseased with an issue, which means she was dealing with something that was impairing her normal function. Something harmful had developed in her. To say it in a very simple way, she was in trouble.

The next thing we see is that this trouble, malfunction, dysfunction, dealt with her blood. If you ever do a study on blood, you will find out the obvious, which is that life is in the blood. The loss of blood can be detrimental to our lives. People's lives are sometimes dependent on whether they can receive a blood transfusion. The blood carries nourishment and oxygen throughout the body. So, no blood, no life. Her blood which should have been circulating and nourishing her is seeping out of her. Her life is seeping out of her. She is being drained, losing her energy, being depleted of her very life. Gradually she is drying up.

This leads us to the third thing we learn about the woman: she had been dealing with this particular issue for twelve long years. This isn't something that happened and was over in a day or a week, not even a month. This issue had lingered on for years. It "took up residence" in her body and in her life and seemed as if it would never go away.

Every day, every month, every year she thought, "Maybe this will be the time that I'll be healed." She didn't just sit by and give up. She made attempts to be healed and whole. She went to doctors and probably tried home-remedies, but nothing worked. In her heart and in her mind, she never gave up. There was a determination in her that somehow, some way she would one day get her desired results. When you consider what she had to face and the time in which she lived, you can see just how much mental strength and inner fortitude she possessed. She was not going to permit this issue, this illness, to win in her life! She wasn't going to allow this limitation to rule her.

In the midst of what she was going through, with all the thoughts of what happened and what didn't happen in the past twelve years, the woman heard something.

She didn't know this something, if she acted on it, would change her life forever. But she knew she had to move out and act on what she heard—that Jesus was passing through where she was. She had heard about Him and how people were healed and made free through His ministry. Her thoughts were not to get Him to come to her house, or to even stop and speak a word to her. She thought, "If I can just get close enough to touch Him, touch His garments, His clothes, I will be healed."

Her faith caused her to eMErge. She didn't care about the naysayers, or the authorities for that matter (because of her condition, she was not allowed to be outside her home or to intermingle with others). Instead, she crawled through the streets and the people and made it to Jesus. In her heart, her faith would not allow her to sit in her home and allow Him to pass by without her even trying. And so, she touched the hem of His garment. Her faith was so pure that Jesus felt virtue leave Him and go to her, healing her in the process. She received what she was longing for. Neither her past nor her present could stop her. She didn't allow it to.

The woman with the issue eMErged because she had to: her very life depended upon whether she pushed through or stayed confined to her home. What are you allowing to confine you? What walls have you built up that are blocking you from receiving what you have been desiring? What are you willing to do to get what you desire? What have you been praying and believing for? Who told you that it was unattainable? And why did you believe them? You can never allow your past to dictate your present or your future. You have to seize every moment! Be alert to the words that you speak to yourself because it's not the outward things that destroy you, it's what happens on the inside. As long as you have breath in your body, it is too soon to give up. Keep breathing, keep believing!

This woman's name was never mentioned but her actions were. She pressed through this difficult time and eMErged into her freedom, a freedom she had a vision of, a freedom she fought hard to attain. She was healed before she touched the hem because of her faith. It may not have been easy, but it was worth it.

Just because you don't have the support group in your corner cheering you on, doesn't mean it's not time for you to eMErge!

What can I do to be a support to myself?

_____

_____

_____

_____

_____

_____

_____

_____

_____

_____

_____

_____

_____

_____

_____

_____

_____

_____

_____

ॐ Day 5 ☙
RAHAB

*And Joshua the son of Nun sent out of Shittim
two men to spy secretly, saying, Go view the land,
even Jericho. And they went, and came into an harlot's
house, named Rahab, and lodged there.*
Joshua 2:1

If you know the story of Rahab in the Bible, the first thing most people would say about her is that she was a prostitute, a whore, a lady of the evening. After reading and studying about Rahab, the first thing I would say is that she was complex. She is one person with many connecting parts that make up a whole. She is not one-dimensional, and she should never be remembered as just the harlot; there is much more to her that what she did. What she did was never who she was. Her vocation was never her profession.

Rahab's story was simple but complicated. She was a harlot who lived in the wall of the city, which means she saw a lot and she knew a lot. When the men of God came knocking at her door, she seized the opportunity. She didn't turn them away or not answer the door, she invited them in and listened to what they had to say. When the enemy showed up to kill the men of God, she hid them and sent the enemy in the opposite direction of where the men of God would be going. Then Rahab gave them instructions on which way they should go and what they might encounter on the way. She also shared with them how long they could stay in those places before the enemy would catch up to them. She was the present help God sent in the time of trouble. Rahab's name means broad, large, boundless and expansive, meaning she had the capacity to "house" the men of God, to aide in saving their lives and ultimately saving her own life and her household.

Can you imagine the rumors and the ridicule she experienced when she allowed the men into her home? The town folk probably were accustomed to her entertaining one gentleman at a time but to allow two men at once and for them to stay? Then she helped them escape with a scarlet rope she tied in her window. This rope is the rope that the men were let down with out of her window and this rope remained in her window for them to see when they returned to destroy the city. it would let them know not to destroy her home or those who were in her household. What kind of foolishness was that? Had Rahab lost her mind? No, this was not foolish; and no, she had not lost her mind. She started gathering family members over to her home to stay. How did she get them to listen to her? You know, I really don't know but I do know that all who listened to her and came to her home, lived! She was trying to save people who knew her, knew her profession and probably did not approve of anything she was doing. The words she spoke though to her family and the men of God must have bypassed their carnal minds and went straight to their spirit because the Bible doesn't mention any of them hesitating to do what she said. They all obeyed and were saved!

No words are written about Rahab changing her profession or becoming a minister that traveled the world but there are words written about her faith. The words stated are these: *By faith the harlot Rahab perished not with them that believed not, when she had received the spies with peace (Hebrews 11:31).* It doesn't say there was a name or job title change, but it does say that because she believed, she did not perish!

EMErging for Rahab was her believing. She believed the good things she heard about God. She believed the miracles, signs, and wonders that had taken place. Because of her belief, nations were saved, and she is included in the lineage of Jesus! She transitioned and eMErged from a place of obscurity; from a place of being seen but not seen, heard but not heard, and being acknowledged for the wrong reasons. The harlot Rahab left a legacy of faith.

When looking at Rahab and her life, we see that no one is beyond God's reach. Despite your messed-up situations or circumstances, God can and will touch you, and minister to you and through you. Living a perfect life is not what He requires from you, only belief. Even in what you consider to be your lowest state or point in life, you can still eMErge!

BELIEVE!!!

How can you start believing in yourself and your own abilities?

ಱ Day 6 ಲ
THE SERVANT GIRL

And the Syrians had gone out by companies,
and had brought away captive out of the land of
Israel a little maid; and she waited on Naaman's wife.
2 Kings 5:2

This young lady was a servant in Naaman's house. She was essentially a slave. Naaman was a foreign ruler who had leprosy and wanted desperately to be healed. The servant girl heard about his sickness; and it is quite possible that she saw him in the midst of what he was going through. While doing her work in the house one day, she mustered up the courage to eMErge. She mentioned to her mistress, Naaman's wife, that she wished her lord would go to the prophet because he would pray for him and he would be healed. This took a lot of courage because she could have easily been reprimanded for speaking up in this situation. She was a servant in the house. She didn't have a voice in the home. Who would listen to a servant girl? Can you imagine the thoughts she had before she said a word? "I know that even though he doesn't serve God, he still can be healed. So, do I say something and risk my own well-being? Will they listen to me? When will I bring this up, how will I bring this up? Am I willing to face what could happen to me and my family?" The possible thoughts are endless.

This servant girl had a true compassion for her master, her lord. She spoke up in a situation that would have normally would have earned her a punishment or even cost her her life. Her master's illness was not shared with her. She saw and she heard and decided to share what she knew would help him. She risked everything so he could be healed.

Take a risk for the right reason!

Emerging Into Your Whole & Beautiful Life

"Sometimes you just have to take the risk." What risk have you taken so someone else could be free? What are you willing to risk so that you can have that same freedom?

_____

_____

_____

_____

_____

_____

_____

_____

_____

_____

_____

_____

_____

_____

_____

_____

_____

ೡ Day 7 ೞ
THE WOMAN WITH AN INFIRMITY

*And, behold, there was a woman
which had a spirit of infirmity eighteen years,
and was bowed together, and could in no wise
lift up herself.*
Luke 13:11

This woman had this infirmity for eighteen years and could in no wise lift herself up. But she was told by Jesus to come to Him. He didn't have anyone bring her to Him, she was asked to come on her own. So, to understand this dilemma, let's look at the word 'infirmity'. It means frailty, weakness, disability, and impairment. This word went against everything the woman could do. She was weak, disabled and frail. It was a task for her to stand, let alone walk. Yet He spoke to her and said, "Come to me."

In that moment, she had a decision to make. She could have complained and gave excuses about why she couldn't get to where Jesus was. She could have gotten angry, thinking, "Jesus knows my condition and yet He is telling me to come to Him. Why won't He come to me?" Sometimes though, you must take a step of faith and that is exactly what she had to do, literally. When she stepped out to walk towards Him, she didn't know whether she would be healed or not. She was simply being obedient.

Through that obedience, she was told to go her way because her faith had made her whole. She wasn't just healed, she was made whole. This wholeness meant she was no longer broken or damaged. She was now sound, intact, and complete, not only in her body, but in her soul and in her spirit. eMErging for her was stepping out on a word and believing that the best could happen for her. It wasn't guaranteed that she would be healed; she didn't know exactly what would happen, but she did it by faith.

Push forward in faith, believe beyond the limitations!

What do you have faith for, the belief that anything can happen? What can you do to "step out" of your comfort zone?

___

ꙮ Day 8 ꙮ
ESTHER

*And he brought up Hadassah, that is, Esther,
his uncle's daughter: for she had neither father nor
mother, and the maid was fair and beautiful; whom
Mordecai, when her father and mother were dead,
took for his own daughter.*
Esther 2:7

Here we meet Esther, a Jewish girl who grows up to become a Queen. Although she became royalty, her eMErging was about continuing to be true to herself, even amidst adversity. Esther was being prepared along with other young ladies to become one of the king's wives. She was being groomed for a position that was uncertain, never knowing whether the role of queen would become hers. God placed her there for a greater purpose than being queen and Esther had to be reminded by her cousin, Mordecai, to remain focused on that true purpose which was to stand in the gap, to pray for her people, the Jews, and to help them receive their freedom. She needed to speak to the king concerning the circumstances surrounding her family and she knew she couldn't approach him—she had to be called in or summoned in to see him. If she went to him without the call, she could lose her life. She prayed about it and came to the conclusion that if she was to die for approaching him, then it would just have to be. She was willing to give her life for her family and for what she believed.

Have you ever been in a situation where you had to make a choice? The choice for YOU? See, in this situation, Esther's ultimate choice was for her. What she chose benefited her kinfolk and her husband, but the choice was for her. Choosing yourself is not about being selfish, but about making a conscious decision knowing that you matter. In the midst of it all, you have to love you enough to fight for you, just like you would fight for a cause or another person.

> ***Every choice is a decision that will determine your destiny!***

Emerging Into Your Whole & Beautiful Life

When you make decisions in this life that you've been given, consider yourself. How do you plan to consider yourself?

_____

_____

_____

_____

_____

_____

_____

_____

_____

_____

_____

_____

_____

_____

_____

_____

_____

༄ Day 9 ༄
HANNAH

*And they rose up in the morning early,
and worshipped before the Lord, and returned,
and came to their house to Ramah: and Elkanah knew
Hannah his wife; and the Lord remembered her.
1 Samuel 1:9*

Hannah's name means favor and grace. It means approved and held in great regard. Hannah was all that, favored by her husband and by God, but she was barren. She could not bear children because her womb was closed. Due to this barrenness, she was ridiculed and talked down upon. This condition had taken her to a place of sadness; some would even say a place of depression. Hannah was always weeping, and she had stopped eating. There was an emptiness in her heart, even knowing that her husband loved her in spite of her being barren.

Can you imagine having favor on your life and you not being able to give life? Think about it: these two things seem to contradict each other. It would seem as though if you were barren then there would be no way favor could be on your life. But in the case with Hannah, she was both favored and barren and she had the grace to walk this journey through until the end.

Her eMErging came when she went to the temple to pray. She stopped gauging her life by what others said or thought about her. She wept and worshipped in the presence of the Lord and she let her request be known. She was specific about what she desired from the Lord, and after she made her request, she went in faith, believing that what she prayed for, she would see it come to pass. Hannah had gotten the release she needed, and she was free.

If you read the story of Hannah, you will see she received the desire of her heart: God granted her the request and she bore a son. Have you ever been in a place where you feel as though you are favored yet you are barren, unfruitful? You may not feel that way now, but one day you will, and the prayer to pray in this place is, "Father, help me to be fruitful in this unfruitful place."

Life can be challenging, but it's for growth, not for you to be depressed or for you to give up.

Desire to be fruitful in barren places.

In what places have you been barren? What steps are you taking to come out of that barren place?

_____
_____
_____
_____
_____
_____
_____
_____
_____
_____
_____
_____
_____
_____
_____
_____
_____
_____
_____

ꙮ Day 10 ꙮ
DAUGHTERS OF ZELOPHEHAD

The daughters of Zelophehad speak right: thou shalt surely give them a possession of an inheritance among their father's brethren; and thou shalt cause the inheritance of their father to pass unto them.
Numbers 27:7

Mahlah, Noa, Hoglah, Milcah, and Tirzah—these five sisters were born at a time where things were not at all favorable for women. They didn't have any brothers so when their father passed away, they were not going to receive their inheritance. During this time in history, the heirs had to be male, so in order to receive an inheritance they had to be married to someone within their father's tribe or other close male relatives would receive the inheritance.

These sisters came together, had a meeting, and concluded that they should be able to receive what rightfully belonged to them, even though the laws at that time were against them. They stood together and approached the counsel, pleaded their case and won!

All of them eMErged from the status quo of their time. It took tremendous courage to fight for what was the right thing to do and for what rightfully belonged to them. Courage is the ability to do something that frightens you. It's a choice and a willingness to confront. These five sisters worked together and pushed through their fears: they had the ability, they made the choice to go forward and they had the willingness to see it through!

Your voice is powerful… Speak up!

Emerging Into Your Whole & Beautiful Life

What is it that you need the courage to confront and conquer? To go beyond the boundaries that others have set? To speak out against an injustice done towards you?

ᚾ Day 11 ᚾ
MARY, THE MOTHER OF JESUS

Now the birth of Jesus Christ was on this wise: When as his mother Mary was espoused to Joseph, before they came together, she was found with child of the Holy Ghost.
Matthew 1:18

Mary's story is unique. You see, this young lady was told by an angel that she was pregnant, and this child would be the Savior of the world. She was about to marry Joseph who had no idea that she would be with child because they had never been intimate. She had not been with another man. Can you imagine the turmoil she was going through? How was she going to tell the man she loved, the man she was engaged to, that she was going to have a baby and that it was by the spirit of God that this happened? She would have to deal with the ridicule of others, thinking she brought shame to her family, to Joseph, and even to herself.

Mary trusted what the angel told her though: do not afraid. She embraced what was said and agreed. Her response to the angel was, "Be it unto me according to thy word." This was a trust beyond her human ability. Trust is assured reliance on the ability, strength, or truth of someone or something. Mary's trust wasn't just in the angel, but in the words the angel spoke, and knowing that all would be well with her, with Joseph and with the baby.

Sometimes situations come where all we can do is trust that the best will come forth. Not all circumstances will look favorable, but there has to be a knowing that it will all work out. She eMErged through her trust. If she didn't trust completely, she might have been passed by instead of being chosen for this great task that would bring forth both turmoil and triumph!

Trust is the willingness to be vulnerable.

Do you have any trust issues? Where did they originate? What are you going to do about building your trust in yourself and others?

ꙭ Day 12 ꙭ
DEBORAH

*And Deborah, a prophetess, the wife of Lapidoth,
she judged Israel at that time.
Judges 4:4*

Deborah was the chosen leader of her time. She was a judge and had to make difficult decisions. Due to the era she lived in, it was rare to have a woman in a leadership position. I imagine that being a leader and a woman was a huge task for her, but she handled it well. Although she may not have been chosen by man, she was chosen, anointed, and appointed by God to accomplish what was set before her.

Deborah was also a prophetess. A prophetess is a female who is regarded as an inspired teacher or proclaimer of the will of God. Being a judge meant she was a public official appointed to decide cases in a court of law. It was awesome that she housed both of these offices and she walked in them with all boldness and authority. She was at peace with who she was called to be. She didn't try to shrink back from her office.

She eMErged through embracing who she was, never putting her focus on what others thought but honing her craft and doing everything she could to be who and what she was called to do and be. Being confident was her strong suit, it was integrated into her being so when she was later called upon to go to war or decide a case, she made the decisions in peace.

__Confidence in yourself will open up many doors of opportunity!__

Emerging Into Your Whole & Beautiful Life

Do you have that one area where you know you are confident in? it could be more than one area. How did you reach that high level of confidence? What area(s) would you like to become more confident in?

_____

_____

_____

_____

_____

_____

_____

_____

_____

_____

_____

_____

_____

_____

_____

_____

_____

_____

_____

ಬ Day 13 ೞ
RIZPAH

And Saul had a concubine, whose name was Rizpah.
2 Samuel 3:7

But the king took the two sons of Rizpah
the daughter of Aiah, whom she bare unto Saul.
2 Samuel 21:8

Rizpah was a concubine of King Saul, meaning she was his "side chick", so to speak. In Biblical times, men had more than one female they were with. She had sons by Saul who were killed simply because of their association with their father. They did not commit a crime or do something wrong.

Rizpah fought for her sons to be taken down off the gallows where they were hung and to be given a proper burial. When she was refused this, she stood guard over her deceased sons' bodies and fought off the birds and other animals that would try to eat their flesh. Rizpah fought over something that seemed to everyone else was dead, but she couldn't allow her sons' lives to be taken for granted and thrown away like they meant nothing. She fought and prayed, prayed and fought, until her sons' bodies were taken down and they were given a proper burial. No, her sons didn't rise from the dead, but she did get some closure and their bodies were buried like they should have been.

Rizpah's tenacity kept her going. She had a determination to stay with the task at hand. People may have told her to go home, your sons are dead, just let it go. The taunting of others could have deterred her or even caused her to have a mental breakdown. She stayed focused and committed to her goal though. Through tiredness, fatigue, hurt, disappointment and so many more emotions, she stood, not wavering. She pushed beyond all her natural abilities to accomplish what she had set out to do; and as she eMErged, nothing and no one could stop her!

Your tenacity is the gift to hold on to something with a firm grip.

Determination makes things happen!

Do you have the tenacity, the determination to see things through until the end? If not, what could you do to develop that type of determination in your life?

ꙮ Day 14 ꙮ
GOMER

The word of the Lord that came unto Hosea,
the son of Beeri, in the days of Uzziah, Jotham,
Ahaz, and Hezekiah, kings of Judah, and in the
days of Jeroboam the son of Joash, king of Israel.
The beginning of the word of the Lord by Hosea.
And the Lord said to Hosea, Go, take unto thee
a wife of whoredoms and children of whoredoms:
for the land hath committed great whoredom,
departing from the Lord. So he went and took
Gomer the daughter of Diblaim; which conceived,
and bare him a son.
Hosea 1:1-3

Gomer was the wife of Hosea the prophet. He was sent to her by divine appointment. She was described as a promiscuous woman, a harlot and a whore. You may say, "Wow, how did she end up with the prophet, the man of God?" Simple: God loved Gomer just as much as he loved Hosea. He desired the best for her because she was His daughter. He loved her, just like He loves us today. And just because Gomer was promiscuous doesn't mean she was unlovable.

However, she had an addiction and it was not easy letting it go. Being a prostitute was not just a job for her, she was addicted to the lifestyle.

If you go back and read the story of Gomer, you will see that even though she had a family and a loving husband who cared for her, her addictive behavior didn't stop. She would run away from her home and go back to that which she was addicted to. She would leave her place of peace, her headquarters, her place of receiving instruction and commands; a place where she needed to receive her strategy for her next move, into a place of anxiety and disarray because of her inner dialogue, because of her feelings of being unworthy and worthless. She was being showered with love, encouragement and support, but she did not receive it!

Yet her husband stayed consistent and persistent in her life. No matter how much she ran away, he would run after her. He never would give up on her. He paid for her, his own wife, so he could get her back and take her home. Gomer's name means complete, whole; and that's what her husband and her heavenly Father wanted her to see. The book of Hosea doesn't reveal Gomer's conclusion. The last scripture that references her is Hosea 3:2-3 where Hosea purchases her and tells her: "You are to live with me many days and you must not prostitute or be intimate with any man and I will behave the same way toward you." I personally believe that Gomer accepted and embraced what Hosea said, realizing that she didn't have to run anymore. In my narrative, she eMErges into a courageous and amazing woman; a beautiful, loyal wife, and a loving and caring mother. She finally connected to herself and realized the very thing that she was searching for was already in her!

Everything I need is in me!

What addiction do you keep running to that your Heavenly Father has paid the price for so you can be free? What is hindering you from receiving unconditional love? All you have to do is receive.

ꙮ Day 15 ꙮ
LEAH

And Laban had two daughters: the name of the elder was Leah, and the name of the younger was Rachel. Leah was tender eyed; but Rachel was beautiful and well favoured.
Genesis 29:16-17

Leah is a woman who is married to a man who doesn't love her. In fact, he is in love with her sister whom he eventually marries as well. Let that sink in. Her husband is in love with another woman and that woman is her sister; and after marrying Leah due to deception, he marries her sister because he is in love. She strives daily to prove to him that she is worthy of his love and that she can be the wife he needs, but no matter what she does, she never wins his heart.

The Father sees that Leah is unloved and opens her womb. She begins to bare children and thinks, "Now my husband is going to love me." She had child after child after child, but her husband still did not love her. Leah had to realize that her marriage, which was based on deception, was never built upon the right foundation. She could not win her husband's love by doing good works. There had to be a relationship, a connection that was beyond the physical as well as an intimacy that was never between them.

Leah had to come to a place within her where she had to shift her focus. Although she still loved her husband, she couldn't depend on him to love her back. So she began to focus on the Lord! She knew that He loved her beyond the conditional love of a man. Since she couldn't develop an intimate relationship with her husband, she developed that relationship with her God! This set her on a path of victory and peace. Leah shifted her focus which means she changed her position and her perception. She went from the position of a victim and the perception of, "If I do this, then my husband will _____." Looking at things from the victim's side, she felt like she was subjected to oppression, hardship and mistreatment. After she came to the end of her victim mentality, she realized that what she was going through did not have to be her plight or her reality. She realized she had a voice and a choice!

The victim is the victor, it's all a matter of perception!

Emerging Into Your Whole & Beautiful Life

Where in your life do you need to shift your focus?

_____
_____
_____
_____
_____
_____
_____
_____
_____
_____
_____
_____
_____
_____
_____
_____
_____
_____
_____
_____
_____

꧁ Day 16 ꧂
HAGAR

Now Sarai Abram's wife bare him no children: and she had an handmaid, an Egyptian, whose name was Hagar. And Sarai said unto Abram, Behold now, the Lord hath restrained me from bearing: I pray thee, go in unto my maid; it may be that I may obtain children by her. And Abram hearkened to the voice of Sarai. And Sarai Abram's wife took Hagar, her maid the Egyptian, after Abram had dwelt ten years in the land of Canaan, and gave her to her husband Abram to be his wife.
Genesis 16:1-3

Hagar is a well-known Biblical character. What we must realize though is that she is just not some personality we read about. She was a woman whose life was turned upside down due to the household she was in. She was a servant in the house of Abraham: Sarah's handmaiden and Abraham's concubine. What is a concubine? A mistress, a woman with whom a man cohabits with but is not married to. The dictionary even describes her as one having a recognized social status in a household below that of a wife. The wife has covenant, the concubine has cohabitation.

Hagar is "the other woman." Sarah hasn't been able to give Abraham children because her womb is closed. She has been told that she would bear children, but she feels like she is too old, so even though she was given this promise by God, she decides to make it happen through other means. Sarah has her handmaiden, her servant, Hagar, go and be physically intimate with Abraham, which results in pregnancy. Sarah thinks this will fulfill the promise, but it doesn't. It only causes hurt and resentment.

After Hagar's son is born, Sarah gets pregnant and also bares Abraham a son. Now she wants Hagar out of their lives. She feels like Hagar's son is receiving more attention than her son and that Abraham cares more for Hagar and her son than her and her son. Can you even begin to imagine how Hagar feels and how she is processing this entire situation? She came into the home as a servant, a handmaid. She worked and did her job well. She became the "second wife", the concubine of Abraham. She was physically intimate with her "master", her employer, without choice, doing as she was told. Only to be put out of the house. Now Hagar and her son are being ostracized, and isolated; because the very one who told her to be intimate with Abraham wants her gone.

Hagar is sent out into the wilderness with her child and there she received the promise. God spoke to Hagar in the wilderness, supplied her immediate need and then let her know that He would make him into a great nation (Genesis 21:17-18). This was her eMErging. She may not have had a covenant, but she had a promise and that covenant, which is a binding agreement, was made for Abraham's seed, not just to his promised seed.

Covenant is covenant, even in the midst of a wilderness.

What is your take on covenant? What part of your life have you been in a wilderness? Can you see the promise in the midst of it all?

_____

_____

_____

_____

_____

_____

_____

_____

_____

_____

_____

_____

_____

_____

_____

_____

_____

_____

ꙮ Day 17 ꙮ
LYDIA

And a certain woman named Lydia, a seller of purple, of the city of Thyatira, which worshipped God, heard us: whose heart the Lord opened, that she attended unto the things which were spoken of Paul. 15 And when she was baptized, and her household, she besought us, saying, If ye have judged me to be faithful to the Lord, come into my house, and abide there. And she constrained us.
Acts 16:14-15

Lydia was a successful businesswoman which was stellar for the era she lived in. The Bible says she was a seller of purple. This speaks of her wealth because dyed cloth was a rare commodity in those days. It is also stated in the Bible that she was a worshipper of God. Notice, it didn't say she accepted Christ as her Savior and Lord, it just says she was a worshipper. This means she had feelings of reverence, adoration, and honor for God but there was no relationship. Because of the reverence she had for God, He was able to touch her heart so that she would be receptive to the teachings of Paul. And through Paul's message, she accepted Jesus into her life as her Lord and Savior and was baptized. She was so excited about her conversion that she couldn't keep silent! She told her family who also gave their lives to Christ.

Although Lydia was successful in a natural sense, she still needed to be successful far beyond what the natural eye could see. She eMErged when she accepted Christ in her life, when she realized that being a successful business woman was only a part of her journey!

Adding relationship to your worship makes the difference!

Where in your life are you honoring God but have not developed a relationship? If you have accepted Christ into your heart, what is your salvation story?

ꙮ Day 18 ꙮ
ANGELA DENISE

Her name means angelic messenger of wisdom, and up until this very moment, that is who she has been and what she's been doing. Her name is not mentioned throughout the Bible, but one particular song describes her life the most and that song is, *This is Me.*

This song speaks about being broken, bruised, and scared, yet accepting all of it. It speaks of being authentically yourself and not being ashamed of who you are. If you haven't figured it out by now, this story, this little snippet, is about yours truly. I believe we all have a story. It's just that not all of us share our story, or we may feel we don't have a platform from which to speak.

My name has always meant angelic messenger of wisdom, but I have not always believed in who I was and what I was destined to do. From as early as I can remember, I have loved to talk, not just for the sake of talking. I also loved researching and finding true and inspiring information and sharing it with others. I would gather information that would help someone or share something with them that they didn't know, or even if they did know maybe adding to their knowledge. This made me happy and excited on the inside. To this very day, I still love to talk and teach but it has not yet become my career, though I would love for it to be. Right now, I process loans for a credit union. I love my job; it has boosted my confidence and for that I am very grateful. But I would also love to be given the opportunity to have a career in speaking and being a bestselling author.

While working this job, life happened, and I had to make some major decisions in what seemed to be the most chaotic time in my life. I had become familiar with and gotten used to being a wife, a mother, and a minister among other roles. Then two of these roles were taken away from me simultaneously and change came to my life.

My eMErging into my whole and beautiful life came at a later age and stage in my life, much later than I anticipated. I thought that when I got married over thirty years ago that it would be forever. I thought that the church I was attending for over fifteen years would be the church I would still be attending and serving in today. These were my thoughts and my heart's desire, but it didn't work out that way. In my latter forties, two of the most important parts of my life were gone and I had to start over, which wasn't and still isn't that easy. I had to reevaluate everything concerning me. What I like, what I didn't like, how to dress, how I wanted to wear my hair, etc. What about my relationship with God? How was I going to sustain and stand when I felt like I had been abandoned?

It took some time, but I was able to pull myself together and start over. It was just a matter of how I perceived my situation. I have friends who told me the truth, they didn't cut corners. They prayed for me, encouraged me and embraced me. I was supported, whether I wanted to be or not. I am still on this path of discovering me, and at this point, I am enjoying every moment. I can't change what happened in my past, but I have a say in what happens in my now and my future!

The word of God says, *Many are the afflictions of the righteous (Psalm 34:19)*, it also says that *God is a present help in the time of trouble (Psalm 46:1)*.

I had to see that even though I was faithful and served God to the best of my ability, it did not exempt me from trouble. I had to grow up some more! I had to have the mentality of, *though he slay me yet will I serve him, yet will I praise Him! (Job 13: 15)* The mindset of, "If He delivers me out of this or even if He doesn't He is still God and I will praise Him, in spite of my situation and my circumstances." eMErging for me is becoming the best ME I can be. It means to authentically, emphatically and undeniably be ME!

The entrance of thy words giveth light; it giveth understanding unto the simple (Psalm 119:130).

Applying the word of God in your everyday life will cause you to grow in your faith and to become mature in your journey. Yes, we can have faith as a mustard seed but even a seed needs to grow and produce. How will you cultivate, nurture, and grow your "seed"?

_____

_____

_____

_____

_____

_____

_____

_____

_____

_____

_____

_____

_____

_____

_____

_____

ॐ Day 19 ॐ
CONFIDENCE

For the Lord shall be thy confidence,
and shall keep thy foot from being taken.
Proverbs 3:26

Confidence is key in eMErging, and it may not be the way you have pictured that it would be. That self-assurance, courage, and boldness may show up in the most uncommon circumstances or situations. It's amazing how differently each one of us may find our way to eMErging. That turning point which will cause, encourage, or push a person past boundaries and limitations. EMErging is not a simple task. It will take tenacity and determination due to the fact you may not have anyone cheering you on through the process. More than likely, no one will be at your "starting line" as you start to push yourself towards your freedom to be the real you.

There is no force behind eMErging—it is a choice; a decision you make. You must take charge of you and allow yourself to walk out the full ongoing process. After one task is accomplished, another one will begin. Each ending leads to a new beginning. The process of coming into full view after being in obscurity for so long may feel uncomfortable but it will be rewarding. Become the star of your own life! Applaud yourself! Embrace yourself! Be your Authentic self!

Emerging Into Your Whole & Beautiful Life

How will you begin to applaud yourself? What are your unique characteristics?

_____
_____
_____
_____
_____
_____
_____
_____
_____
_____
_____
_____
_____
_____
_____
_____
_____
_____

ꙮ Day 20 ꙮ
WRITE YOUR OWN STORY

*For I know the thoughts that I think toward you,
saith the Lord, thoughts of peace, and not of evil,
to give you an expected end.
Jeremiah 29:11*

Give a brief synopsis of your own story. What have you learned so far in your journey?

_____

_____

_____

_____

_____

_____

_____

_____

_____

_____

Emerging Into Your Whole & Beautiful Life

ꙮ Day 21 ꙮ
CONNECTION

*And beside this, giving all diligence, add to your
faith virtue; and to virtue knowledge; And to knowledge
temperance; and to temperance patience; and to patience
godliness; And to godliness brotherly kindness; and to
brotherly kindness charity. For if these things be in you,
and abound, they make you that ye shall neither be
barren nor unfruitful in the knowledge of
our Lord Jesus Christ.
2 Peter 1:5-8*

There is a common thread in each one of the women we discussed: they decided to LIVE and eMErge. Their situations and circumstances may not have been the best or the same. The environments they were placed in may not have been favorable, but they decided to be free, prosperous and productive in the place they were in, whether it was thriving or dry. The key is never to allow your outside to determine your inside. Get things stable on the inside and you will begin to flourish on the outside. When you change your mind, you change your life. And when you think differently, you become different.

Have you ever seen a flower push through a crack in the sidewalk or grow in a place where normally it would perish? Somehow, some way it maneuvered its way to the sunlight! You may think your dream has died…not so! You may think that it's too late…not so! All it takes is for you to decide to push through to transition to eMErge! Nothing is impossible to those who believe. So, are you believing in You? If no one else does, you must. You need to be your own cheerleader with pompoms and all.

This life is what you make of it. Things and people can and will change in a moment, but there must be a consistency. Take charge of you. Invest in you, your now and your future. You are worth it, flaws and all. You are FLAWESOME—despite every flaw you may have, you are still amazing and extraordinary.

Perfection is not needed for you to eMErge and to be whole and beautiful; all you need is determination, discipline and a knowing on the inside that you are worth the journey. You have stood with others and poured your time and energy into helping them attain their dreams. Now you need to do the same for you. Take the time to invest in you and evolve into the best person you can be! Start allowing your dreams and visions to become your reality. Speak life to yourself, encourage yourself, release yourself, gauge yourself, and enhance yourself. Give yourself permission to be totally free to be who you are destined to be. No limitations!

It Is Time To EMERGE Into Your Whole And Beautiful Life!

Emerging Into Your Whole & Beautiful Life

What connections or steps do you need to make to assist you in making your dream a reality? Set your goals and make a timeline.

_____

_____

_____

_____

_____

_____

_____

_____

_____

_____

_____

_____

_____

_____

_____

_____

_____

_____

_____

_____

_____

ꙮ DECISIONS ☙

Life can be challenging, and it can also be a struggle, but those challenges and struggles should only cause us to strengthen ourselves and excel. It really has to deal with how we process our life experiences. Life is what we make of it, so now is the time for you to make your life beautiful! Walk out the process that will make your life whole, prosperous and productive. It's time to face your own self in the mirror and make the decisions needed to cause your life to be what has always been in your heart. Live your dream on purpose and live a purposeful life.

How can you do it, you may ask. Well, it's simple—make a decision and stick with it. Follow it through. Oftentimes decisions and thoughts are in our minds but the commitment to walk it out never comes. Once a decision is made and it is coupled with commitment, it becomes a recipe for change. Plans must be made, goals need to be set and deadlines have to be met, so that dream, that vision will become a reality. You are the only one who can stop your progress. No one else has that kind of power unless you give it to them.

Emerging Into Your Whole & Beautiful Life

Everything may not line up the way you desire it to, but so what? No excuses! You have got to learn how to push beyond the push and how to stand when you feel like sitting down and giving up. We all need to know how to reach beyond the ordinary into the extraordinary. Everyday opportunities are given but how many are taken? When will the limitations come off your life? When will your capacity be enlarged? Life can be as big or as small as you desire. The decision is yours. Just know a decision can not only change individual lives, it can change other people's lives as well. The decision to finally start your own business opens job opportunities for others. The decision to go to college to get a bachelor's, master's, or doctorate degree opens doors for you, which can then open doors for others. The decision to stop by a particular store on the way home may cause you to cross paths with a person who needs someone to talk to, who needs prayer or an encouraging word. You are just one decision away from your destiny, your miracle, the most amazing life imaginable! Again, the decision is yours to make.

Angela D. Oliphant

Emerging Into Your Whole & Beautiful Life

ଔ POEM ଓ

Today I went to a funeral
Just to say goodbye
Knowing there would be no resuscitation or
bringing back to life
All the memories seem to overtake me
Flooding me all at once – remembering, pondering-
releasing and letting go
I have to so I can move forward
To attain the prize that lies ahead
Today I went to a funeral
Not many people were there
Just the ones who gave you life
So excited, enthusiastic, full of joy and love, in complete
awe of your existence-
Enamored about what would become
As time went by you started to fade and I watched you
drift slowly away- I said
Goodbye long before your death
Jolted me with dismay
But here I am at this funeral and I really dislike long
goodbyes so I must
Let you go quickly do my 180 and swiftly walk away…
because life as

Angela D. Oliphant

I have known it has drifted and slipped through my hands like sand

I can't find the individual particles to ever put things together again
So I say goodbye to you for now, until we meet again –
until I walk down life's
Aisle and come face to face with you again
Goodbye to you as I heal
Goodbye to you as I'm mended
Goodbye to you as I am restored, rejuvenated and reimagining me
Putting the pieces back together again
Replenishing- doing life without you- embracing me

Today I went to the funeral
Although it was not my choice
Situations, circumstances, played out like a symphony, brought me to this place
Even though this was not the song – I wanted to hear or play

Today I went to a funeral, but I refused to die
Because I have the desire to live and press forward with my life
What happened is a tragedy
But new growth will come
Because this funeral is just a ceremony- not my finale'
A giant leap into my destiny
A ray of light upon my path

Emerging Into Your Whole & Beautiful Life

A leaving behind – a reaching towards – the greatest opportunity I've ever had

So today I honor these 29 years 2 months and 8 days that have truly blessed my life- my marriage is done

I bid thee farewell – it's been nice, I've learned, and I've grown and now it's time for the final curtain call – so, so long my dear friend – Auf wierdersen – Good bye!

Angela D. Oliphant

ACKNOWLEDGEMENT

I am so blessed to have so many awesome women in my life that have loved me, encouraged me and supported me.

THANK YOU!

Make sure you love and support the women in your life!

Angela D. Oliphant

ꙮABOUT THE AUTHORꙮ

Angela D. Oliphant is, at heart, a teacher. She grew up in the small town of Aiken, South Carolina and she always had dreams that took her further than the boundaries where she physically lived.

Angela has always had a love for words because through them she saw and experienced life in a whole new light. Early in her life, she realized words could transform, train and equip every person who would take the time to read and embrace them—whether through books, magazines, or even a newspaper. With this passion and thirst to help others understand the wealth found in words, she has set out on a mission to teach, train and equip all who will listen and apply words to their lives that will bring order in the midst of chaos and calm in the midst of any storm. She believes that the right words spoken at the right time in the lives of others can elevate their thinking to the place where there are no limitations or boundaries to what they want to accomplish in their lives.

Through poetry, short stories, articles, and public speaking—she has presented opportunities that will bring a positive change to the lives of all who will listen and understand that their entire world can literally be transformed "One Word at a Time."

Email address: wholebeautiful@gmail.com
Facebook: Whole & Beautiful
Instagram: wholeandbeautiful

www.ingramcontent.com/pod-product-compliance
Lightning Source LLC
Chambersburg PA
CBHW021118080526
44587CB00010B/566